Boss is hungry

By Debbie Croft

Boss is my dog.

Boss is hungry.

Here is the food.

Here is the water.

Here is a bone.

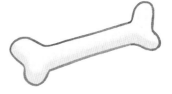

The food goes here
in the little bowl.

The water goes here
in the big bowl.

The bone goes here
on the grass.

Look at Boss.

Boss is not hungry.

Boss is playing.

Boss is asleep.